About the author's work as mentor.

"Also, just wanted to say thanks for all the help, this was a strange and very new experience for me and I valued your help very much." Nigel N.

"Thanks so much for your excellent advice and guidance during the last few months reference getting our business up and running, it's been much appreciated by both my brothers and myself." Chris E.

"Many thanks for helping me to make my idea become reality. God bless you." Ben G.

"Thank you for all your help with getting this business off the ground" Kara H.

"The great difficulty lies in making it simple."

John Dryden

Be Your Own Marketing Guru

From First Principles To First Customers: A DIY Workbook

David Chapple

To Katie

Contents

Introduction

Let's Generate Some I.P.

WARNING: This workbook contains no advice!

Instead, we are going to do something pragmatic together to create intellectual property - in other words, 'know-how' that only you will have.

Physics tells us that it takes a lot of energy to get a mass moving, but once it's gained momentum, it takes less energy to maintain its movement forwards. Initiating a business should be thought of in the same way. You need to focus your available resources in one direction only, and with one aim: to get sustainable momentum. It's not the time for trial-and-error and *hope-for-the-best*.

Let's address the obvious. There's already a mountain of marketing advice out there for new businesses, yet the hard truth is this: most new businesses fail within three years. Technical start-ups face even steeper odds.

You've probably heard the advice to "know your customer" and "identify their pain points". It's correct and easy to say, but for new businesses it's often frustratingly abstract. We have spent a lot of time thinking about our business already, and given the weight of our unique knowledge, it will take us more effort than anyone else to put ourselves in our customer's shoes and think from both points of view.

And how can you know your customers when you don't have any yet? How do you meaningfully articulate their pain points, so they become useful? How do you do all this without tools? And how do you know if what you have is complete?

The principles here are grounded in experience, shaped by mentoring people in a government programme for new businesses. When the question "How will you get customers?" came up it was surprising how little thought was given to it. Vague answers were often accepted without challenge, even by loan providers, as though customers would magically appear.

Business plans were peppered with hope rather than actionable strategies. A common refrain would be, "I'll start with family and friends and grow through word of mouth." It sounds logical, even comforting, but you could be betting on a false dawn.

Compare that to a plan designed to reach total strangers - the elusive, cold customers who don't know you exist and are totally preoccupied with other stuff. They're the ones you need when family and friends have done their bit. So why not start with them?

At the end of using this workbook, I hope you'll be left with actionable insights - intellectual property to draw upon that results in sales from cold customers. You wouldn't be starting a business if you didn't have vision and energy. If this workbook provides just one answer that brings focus and removes any hope-for-the-best from the plan, then it might have done its job.

But obviously, I hope we achieve a lot more than that.

The Challenge

Here's the task: you are to take people - your future customers - on a journey that begins with them knowing nothing about you, and which ends with them buying your product or service. That's no small feat. If things go well, the relationship won't stop there, but let's agree this initial transformation is the challenge we're taking on.

Taking someone on this journey isn't just about catchy slogans or clever ads. It's about changing minds - literally. As people engage with your messaging, their brains undergo physical changes. Synapses form, breakfast turns into repurposed proteins which become neural connections, and brain chemistry fizzes to build new thoughts and associations.

This mental effort is hard work. The easier you make it, the more likely they are to stay on your path. If we do this right, the result will be *measurable behavioural change*. In other words, we are not just going to change their minds, we'll be able to tell we have, because their behaviour changes in a way that is *testable*. To put it another way, one moment the prospect wasn't doing something, but now they are! The best example is when a prospect wasn't buying our offering, but they turn into a customer. That's a solid behavioural change that can be measured by examining the accounts or witnessing the customer putting their hand in their pocket to pay.

The behavioural change might be more subtle, of course. For instance, whereas your prospect may have been silent, they now are nodding or asking a question. Either way, we're looking to achieve behavioural change that's obvious. So obvious, you can hit it with a stick.

Don't actually do that.

AIDA - an Introduction

To guide your audience on their cognitive journey, we need a proven pathway.

Enter AIDA: This stands for:

- Attention
- Interest
- Desire
- Action

This classic model has stood the test of time. Each stage builds on the one before to drive the desired outcome. We aim to create a journey that is well-formed.

As you can imagine, we need to get people's attention first. This is a distinct effect that we can have on people's brains, and we'll talk more about it later.

Once we have their attention, then we will need to interest them in our offering and generate desire. These two are separate cognitive processes, and we need to activate the parts of the brain that deal with them.

Lastly, we need to get them to take action of some sort. It might be to press a button on a website, scan a QR code, swipe a payment card, or book us in to start the work.

We are dealing with a very organic situation of course, so let's not expect to do things in a strict order. To explain, I'll use an analogy from rail travel.

Imagine two parallel railway tracks with two stations, one at each end. Each track has its own platform at the start and finish. Two trains, Interest and Desire run on these tracks and while both trains start from the same station, they can depart independently of each other. They also arrive at the destination in their own time too.

In our analogy, getting Attention is the moment when either train can depart. It's the signal that one of them should. It's really an event, rather than a stage, as suggested by AIDA. Imagine someone blowing a whistle.

If you sell jewellery, Desire is probably initiated first. That's because you may have used an image of the item in a beautiful setting so that the viewer is attracted by the imagery.

If you sell training courses, then Interest is probably initiated first. That's because you may have triggered a cognitive interest to know more with a challenging hook.

Both trains must make their way to the destination, perhaps running side by side at times, and when both trains have come to the end of their journey, then Action can happen. See Action as another moment but this time a photographer's flash goes off.

When we are marketing, which is a remote, broadcast process, we will only know if our prospects have taken action by the results that come through. We count the flashes. When we are selling, which is a personal process, we're involved in making sure the flash happens.

We are going to tease all of this apart and leave you with actionable assets that make this system work, and which are specific to your business.

Process vs Product

You might also be interested to know that, instead of adopting a process-based approach, we take a product-based approach.

A process-based approach would be where I suggest what you should do.

Compare this to a product-based approach where our objective is for you to create useful things, assets or 'products'. These things could be just words or images on paper, but they are unique to you, they exist in their own right, and they have value. Again, the 'hit it with a stick' test applies. It's not the same if I give you advice or tell you what to do.

These products will hopefully be assets that give impetus to your marketing decisions and future activity. You can use them to your advantage in your sales and marketing in any way that you see fit. You know your business after all.

Why is this product vs process distinction important? Consider the difference between two different workers at a fast-food restaurant. They each have a different, but simple instruction:

- Serve customers and take payments.
- Create delighted customers.

One is about doing i.e. a process-based instruction, and the other is about the end result, which is a product-based instruction. As you may have spotted, notions of completion and quality seem built-in to the product-based approach. These are the elements that are missing in the 'just do it' approach.

The second employee is treated as wise and trusted to do what is required, to bring their personal resources to the job and to work out the 'how' for themselves.

You may be surprised to know how common it can be for humans do their jobs, or any activity, thinking in terms of process. There's a whole

project management methodology founded on the difference. That's because it is easier to think in terms of processes and 'doing'. For instance, it is easier to do the weekly shopping than it is to think about and buy the ingredients for a meal. Product-based thinking takes more cognitive effort.

Customers think in terms of the end product and quality, not what your business actually does to get there. Imagine someone at a repair kiosk waiting for their shoes to be re-soled. While the technician works, the customer may find something to do on their phone instead of making sure the repair process is being conducted to their satisfaction. All the customer really wants is their shoes back and to know the repair will last.

So, if your thinking becomes product-centric, you become customer-centric too.

In taking a product-based approach, we start with the principle that you are wise, and you know about your business. This workbook can only ask good questions and so its effect is open-ended and unconstrained.

The Socratic Method

Background

The Socratic method - a cornerstone of classical education - is built on the power of questions. Its purpose is to lead someone out of their current understanding and into new insights.

The word "educate" itself comes from the Latin *ex-* (out of) and *ducere* (to lead). The question-and-answer process involves the student *actively,* and that activity works to embed the subject. We're in the business of building synapses after all, and we need the student to be properly involved (starting with breakfast).

Compare that to another model where I just 'tell you', and you passively observe. It's like trying to fill a water bottle with a hose from a distance. Not a lot goes in.

This workbook uses the Socratic approach to spark discovery. By asking informed, carefully crafted questions, you'll uncover valuable insights about your audience. These questions are rooted in disciplines like business analysis, marketing, and social science, providing a structured way to think about your customers and your approach to reaching them.

In face-to-face mentoring, this process often creates moments of clarity - for both the mentor and the client. Something that once seemed insignificant suddenly clicks into place, revealing its importance in the bigger picture. The ultimate payoff? That 'lightbulb' moment when everything falls into place.

A Real-World Example

Consider a language school owner working through a "know your customer" exercise. She holds classes for students in a private venue.

In session, she realised that most of her students were males who were business professionals aiming for promotion, while a smaller group consisted of younger learners whose parents footed the bill.

So, while keeping her class sessions in place and maintaining her charges for them, she made the following changes to her business:

- She offered one-on-one sessions in informal settings like cafés and galleries, giving her clients practical, real-world language practice.
- She charged a different rate for these sessions to reflect the value her professional clients perceived.
- She distributed business cards in office kitchens, directly reaching her ideal audience.

Getting the Most Out of This Workbook

It's assumed you're very busy and preoccupied, and by necessity, probably a bit impatient. This workbook is deliberately 'bare bones' to make the best use of your time and energy. What follows is a series of worksheet exercises, each one preceded by a short explanation.

Just so you know how much time is involved, if we were to work through these exercises in a workshop, we'd need to spend a full day together.

1 There are no wrong answers

This isn't a test, a questionnaire, or a magazine quiz where you're chasing a score.

The questions asked are really prompts to provoke thought. They are intended to provide structure and help ensure you consider all options. Your considered, genuine responses are what matter. So, if you can, take time to explore and reflect.

If you do this, every answer is a right answer.

2 Work through the sheets in order

Many worksheets rely on preceding ones, so generally, you should start at the beginning and work your way through.

However, different people work in different ways and we don't want to be rigid or prescriptive. If you need to make several passes through the workbook, or return to previous worksheets, do whatever works for you.

I do have a special request though. Please do the first two exercises without reading ahead.

3 Collaborate

We aren't working together, so, if possible, involve someone else in this process. Their role is to discuss options with you and challenge any assumptions you might not realise you're making. A second perspective can be invaluable.

4 Our A to B journey

As mentioned, most marketing starts with your customer. We, however, are going to use your product or service as the starting point for our investigation, and from there, find out about your prospective customers.

We'll assume you do not have any customers yet.

5 Where the Science comes from

The research behind these worksheets comes from various sources and they'll be credited. You'll see references every now and then, and I have put the notes at the end. There won't be a lot of detail since this is 'bare bones', but the signposts are there if you want to find out more.

If you want to make a note of search terms to follow up on later, you'll find space for them at the back too.

6 Grab a note pad

This workbook is intended for a wide range of scenarios and readers, which means the space provided for your responses gives no clue to how long or short your responses should, or could, be.

Therefore, you might want to grab a note pad and use it when your thoughts need to spill over.

Each exercise is numbered for you, so you can collate your notes.

OK. Are you ready? Let's go!

About You and Your Company

Your Company Slogan

Let's imagine you have a company van or truck, and you are going to have a slogan sign-written on the side. It will appear with your business name and contact details.

If you prefer, imagine that you are going to have some business cards printed urgently, and you need to brief the printer with your instructions now.

Don't worry if your business type wouldn't ordinarily have a slogan. Do it anyway. If you have one already, please use that.

You are being asked to do this as part of a later test to see if you change your thoughts. We'll come back to this at the end of the workbook to check.

Exercise 1

Write your company name, and then a slogan underneath it.

Notable Things About You

Please make a bullet-point list of things about you, using the prompts to provoke responses. Include anything notable. Don't worry about the order, it can be totally random.

To show that just bullets are needed, and by way of example, Einstein might have started his list like this:

- Violin
- German (ex), Swiss, American
- Husband, father, stepfather
- 2 mountains named after me
- Public Speaker
- Refugee
- Physics

... and so on. Here are some prompts:

- Hobbies and leisure activities, interests, and passions
- Experiences, major life events, challenges overcome, accomplishments
- Skills and talents
- Little known facts about you, hidden talents
- Quirks, traits, characteristics
- Groups and community involvement, volunteering and philanthropy, teaching, and mentoring
- Jobs, work, and career
- Education and training
- Specialist knowledge

You'll need your list later in a way that I hope will surprise you. Be sure to come back here to add things as they occur to you. You'll probably be up a ladder or just nodding off to sleep at the time.

Exercise 2

Write your list below.

Your Trust Framework

Trust is the foundation of any successful business relationship. Identify the specific actions, qualities and practices that make your business dependable in the eyes of your customers. Each layer of the framework represents a different facet of trust.

Top: Loyalty Builders

These are the extra touches that turn one-time customers into repeat clients or advocates.

- What unique or personal touches do you provide?
- How do you go above and beyond?

Middle: Security

These are actions or policies that make customers feel safe choosing your business.

- What reassurances do you offer?
- What policies or guarantees show customers you stand behind your work?
- How do you handle mistakes or concerns?

Base: Reliability

These are your essential practices that ensure customers can depend on you.

- What systems or processes guarantee consistent results?
- What basic promises do you always keep?
- Do you have any certifications or industry awards?

Exercise 3

Write your trust builders below.

Your Offering

The Features of Your Offering

Think about the features of your product or service that your customers can easily perceive and understand - these are the aspects they'll notice and care about. You might also include features you want to highlight in your messaging. Here are some simple examples:

For a gutter clearing service:

- Gutter clearance
- Down pipes checked and unblocked
- Wiping the surrounding paintwork

For a voucher app:

- Self-registration
- Access to an existing audience
- Real-time expiry metrics

For an office chair:

- Height adjustable
- Lumbar support
- Large, carpet-friendly wheels
- Padded arm rests
- Steel frame construction

In the space, list the key features of your offering. These should reflect what you want your customers to know about, and what they'll find useful or valuable. Bullet points are just fine. This is a key exercise, so for best results do not move on until you are happy that your list is complete.

Exercise 4

List the features of your offering.

MOSCOW

Let's look at how your audience will respond emotionally to your offering and features, and justify their choice.

I've borrowed the MoSCoW scale, which stands for *Must Have, Should Have, Could Have* and *Would Like to Have.*

Your audience's view of your offering or features governs how you should present it. For example, jewellery is a *Would like to have* so it needs beautiful imagery and aspirational text to work. A first-aid kit is a *should have* for many people.

Must Have

The Domain of Survival and Risk Avoidance

'Must Have' offerings and features appeal to the reptilian brain, which governs instinctive survival needs and threat avoidance. These elements are perceived as critical, and the absence of a 'Must Have' may evoke anxiety or fear of negative consequences.

Example Justifications

Risk Mitigation: Customers choose 'Must Haves' to avoid potential harm, loss, or failure.

Basic Functionality: The features are the foundation of the product's purpose and ensure it works as expected.

Trust and Reliability: Without the features, the product or service would fail to inspire confidence.

Emotional Appeal

The emotional connection for 'Must Haves' is rooted in fear, security, and reassurance. Customers feel safe, in control, and confident when these needs are met.

When Marketing

Stress the Essentials: Position the 'Must Have' as the cornerstone reason to buy.

Should Have

The Domain of Logic and Rational Decision-Making

'Should Have' offerings and features appeal to the neocortex - the rational, analytical part of the brain. These elements are seen as important because they make logical sense, offer a business case, a clear value, and a positive cost/benefit ratio.

Example Justifications

Efficiency and Productivity: Your offering makes the customer more effective or saves time and resources.

Value for Money: Customers see your offering as necessary for maximising their investment.

Competitive Edge: They elevate the customer above their competitors.

Emotional Appeal

The emotional connection for 'Should Haves' is tied to confidence, satisfaction, and empowerment from making a smart, rational choice.

When Marketing

Show the Value: Demonstrate how your offering improves the customer's efficiency or effectiveness.

Could Have

The Domain of Potential and Opportunity

'Could Have' offerings or features spark curiosity and appeal to the creative and exploratory parts of the brain. These are appreciated for the possibilities they open up, the novelty or incremental improvement they bring. This appeals to the part of the brain involved in imagination, problem-solving, and long-term planning.

Example Justifications

Flexibility and Futureproofing: Customers may see these features as adding versatility or adaptability to a product. It's about leaving room for growth or unforeseen needs.

Curiosity and Exploration: 'Could Have' elements tap into a desire to try something new or explore an unexpected benefit, appealing to the human love of discovery and innovation.

Unarticulated Needs: Sometimes, customers don't realise they might need or want a feature until they encounter it. 'Could Have' features give them that "aha!" moment.

Emotional Appeal

The emotional connection for 'Could Have' items is often linked to feelings of possibility, creativity, and self-improvement. They signal opportunity and inspire customers to imagine what they could achieve or experience with the offering.

When Marketing

Focus on Possibilities: Position your features as opening doors to new opportunities or ways to use the product.

Would Like to Have

The Domain of Emotion and Luxury

'Would Like to Have' offerings or features appeal to the mammalian brain, which governs emotions, social status, and pleasure. These elements create a sense of indulgence, exclusivity, or self-expression, making them desirable.

Example Justifications

Emotional Fulfilment: Customers choose these features to feel joy, excitement, or indulgence.

Status and Prestige: These elements help people stand out or express their identity.

Pure Enjoyment: They provide non-essential but highly valued pleasure.

Emotional Appeal

The connection for 'Would Like to Haves' is tied to delight, pride, and aspiration. Customers feel rewarded or special when they indulge in these features.

When Marketing

Appeal to Aspirations: Position these features as tools for self-expression or achieving a dream.

Exercise 5

How do you think your customers will view your complete offering?

Exercise 6

Now, revisit your features, and annotate each one with a MoSCoW tag (M, S, C, W) to say how you think your audience will judge it (and to inspire your thinking on how you might market it).

Your Customer's Hot Buttons

Hot Buttons

This is a technique to help uncover the benefits of your offering and your audience's hot buttons.

Hot buttons are the emotional benefits that can trigger a buying decision. They answer the critical question: *"What's in it for me (that could make me happier)?"*

Rather than leaving this to guesswork, this method ensures your list of hot buttons is thorough, accurate, and impactful.

So, how do we do this?

We keep prompting ourselves with:

> *"... which means that ..."*

Start with one of the features you identified in Exercise 4 and append the phrase "... which means that ..." to it. Hopefully, the response will be a benefit.

Then repeat this process, each time adding *"...which means that..."*. Uncover a new benefit, until you arrive at one or more benefits that have a strong emotional pull. These emotionally resonant benefits are your hot buttons.

On the right is an example for some accounting software. The circles in the chain represent "... which means that ...". So, the first lines read like this:

Amounts are entered only once, which means that there are no copying errors, which means that the accounts always balance ...

... and so on.

Note that your customers' pain points can be calculated from the benefits and hot buttons by working out the inverse. So instead of saying *'I get to leave work on time'* you get a pain point of *'I have to work late to find errors'*. I've added this to the chain at the bottom, and you can do the same in your responses too.

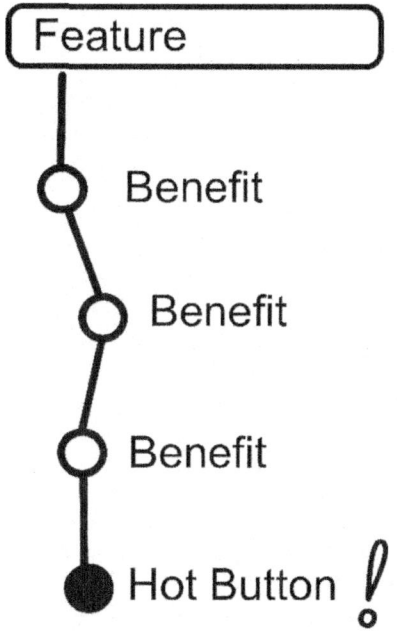

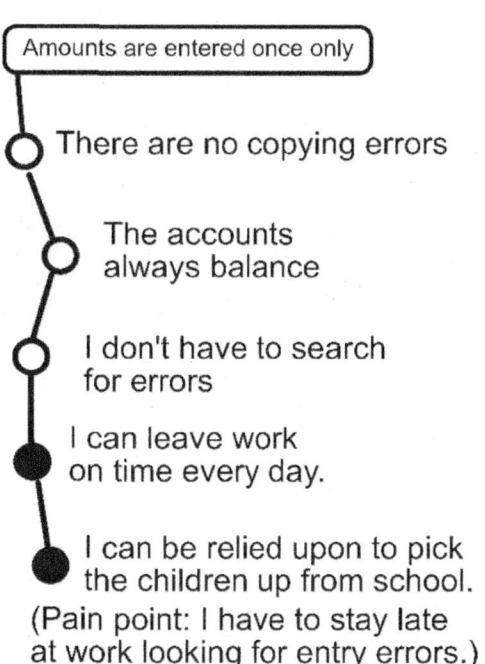

Now it's your turn. Have you got your first feature in mind?

Let's go!

Exercise 7

For each of your features, work out the benefits, hot buttons and if you wish, pain points.

Exercise 8

In the space below and in as few words as possible, can you articulate the main pain point that your whole offering addresses? (You'll need this later).

Your Customer's Needs

Needs Analysis

Here's some information to prepare you for the next section. We are going to explore the *needs* your audience have for your offering.

Instead of plucking them straight out of the air, we'll use a generic list of needs and see which of those are addressed by your offering. In this way, we'll be able to generate a complete list, and maybe uncover some surprises on the way.

You have just made a list of features, so it will be interesting to see if you use them all. Or perhaps you have some features you didn't think were worth mentioning but which turn out to be important. Let's find out.

We'll use Maslow's Hierarchy[1]. This divides generic human needs into eight types, and they are processed from the bottom, up.

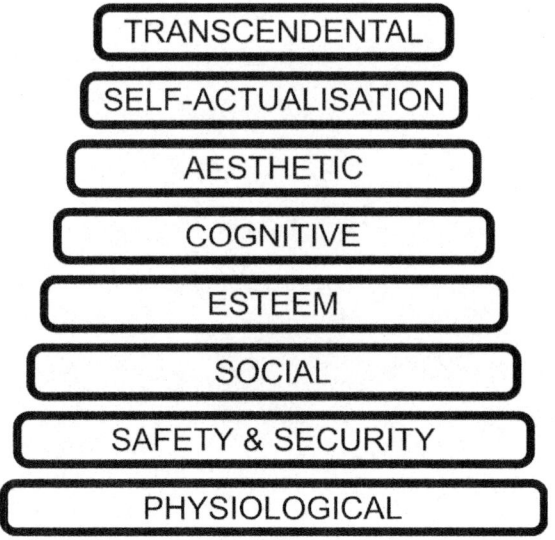

TRANSCENDENTAL

SELF-ACTUALISATION

AESTHETIC

COGNITIVE

ESTEEM

SOCIAL

SAFETY & SECURITY

PHYSIOLOGICAL

The bottom-up structure of Maslow's Hierarchy reflects the order that needs are satisfied in. If a need at one level is not met, then we won't be interested in satisfying the ones above it.

For example, if our security needs are not being met, we'll want to resolve that as a priority, and we won't be so interested in organising a party, reading a book or buying a painting.

Your Solutions

There are eight worksheets, one for each of Maslow's generic needs. Each need is described in more detail there.

Our aim is to identify specific needs (as prompted by each worksheet) and say *how your offering addresses each one*. Hopefully, you will end up with a complete list, and a solid picture of your offering as a solution.

You can do this in a sentence if you like, like the ones following. The first two are from a gutter clearing company.

"We satisfy our customers' need for reassurance that we are doing a great job by taking before-and-after videos by drone."

"To ensure that rodents cannot enter their loft space, we always check for fresh activity and possible entry points during our paintwork wipe-down."

Those examples would probably appear in the *Security* worksheet. Here's one for a dining club app, which would appear in the *Esteem* worksheet.

"For people who wish to make connections in their community, we bring like-minds together for dinner."

Consumer or Organisation

You might provide services or products to people, or to organisations like companies or charities. Or you may supply both people and organisations.

Organisations have needs as well, and as our categories are generic, it follows that their needs fit into the same categories as those that people have. So you'll find two prompts in each exercise. The second explanation could help you identify the extra needs your buyers may have if they represent an organisation as well.

Offering or Feature?

When thinking about how your offering addresses a need, you might want to refer to your whole offering, or a feature.

Also, your offering might address just one need, but, be prepared for it to touch on several.

Identifying the need is much more important than deciding where it goes. Here are some examples to show the kind of variety possible:

Insurance may focus solely on customers' *security* needs and just two features might be mentioned:

- payouts when there's a loss of some kind
- monthly payments

A gym membership on the other hand might address:

- physiological (health)
- *social* (community)
- *esteem* (achievement) needs.

A coffee shop however can have a lot of features which arguably cover a wide range of needs, as follows:

- *physiological* (providing food and drinks)
- *safety* (offering a comfortable and public space)
- *social* (facilitating interaction with others)
- *esteem* (allowing customers to identify with a social culture or to be seen in a group)
- *cognitive* (providing a place to work or read)
- *aesthetic* (featuring appealing furniture and décor)
- *self-actualisation* (supporting the customer's self-image of belonging to a café society)

About your Features

At the end of the next eight worksheets, you might want to revisit your feature list to see if any have been missed out from this exercise.

Physiological (The Basics of Survival)

If you sell to people

At the lowest level are physiological needs like food, water, and shelter - essentials for survival. Without these, an individual cannot function or focus on higher-level goals. Meeting these needs is the first step toward stability and well-being.

If you sell to organisations

The equivalent would be basic operational needs like cash flow, essential utilities, and functional infrastructure needed for survival. These are the bare necessities for an organisation to stay viable, such as paying for electricity, rent, employee salaries, and inventory.

Exercise 9a

Note the basic survival needs that you address, and say how.

Safety (Security and Protection)

If you sell to people

Security and safety needs are derived from a person's environment. Once physiological needs are met, individuals seek safety and security. This includes physical safety (freedom from harm), financial stability (steady income, savings), health, and a predictable environment. Safety fosters a sense of order and allows people to plan for the future.

If you sell to organisations

For an organisation, the equivalent of safety and security may mean financial stability, legal compliance, and risk management, as well as physical security. This includes having a solid business plan, insurance, secure contracts, and measures to protect against fraud or market fluctuations.

Exercise 9b

Note the security and protection needs that you address, and say how.

Social (Belonging and Connection)

If you sell to people

People need emotional connections with others. Humans are inherently social beings. At this level, individuals yearn for meaningful relationships - friendships, family bonds, and romantic connections. Feeling accepted and valued within social groups provides emotional support and combats isolation.

If you sell to organisations

The equivalent is customer relationships, team collaboration, and partnerships. An organisation needs to foster positive connections with customers, build a strong team culture, and establish meaningful industry partnerships.

Exercise 9c

Note the belonging and connection needs that you address, and say how.

Esteem (Respect and Recognition)

If you sell to people

Esteem needs reflect a desire for achievement and recognition. This includes self-esteem (confidence, independence) and external validation (status, respect from others). Meeting these needs boosts personal worth and motivation to strive for more.

If you sell to organisations

The equivalent is reputation, brand image, and market position. Gaining recognition in the industry, being trusted by customers, and achieving respect from competitors are key goals at this level. If your product or service satisfies this need, then how?

Exercise 9d

Note the respect and recognition needs that you address, and say how.

Cognitive (Knowledge and Understanding)

If you sell to people

Beyond basic and social needs, individuals seek intellectual stimulation and a deeper understanding of the world. This involves curiosity, problem-solving, learning new skills, and exploring ideas. Cognitive fulfilment drives innovation and growth.

If you sell to organisations

The equivalent is learning, innovation, and market insight. To grow and adapt, businesses need to invest in understanding their market, analysing data, and staying informed about trends and new technologies.

Exercise 9e

Note the knowledge and understanding needs that you address, and say how.

Aesthetic (Appreciation of Beauty)

If you sell to people

Aesthetic needs relate to the appreciation of beauty, symmetry, and harmony. This can involve enjoying art, music, nature, or creating something meaningful. Satisfying these needs enhances an individual's quality of life.

If you sell to organisations

The equivalent can be design, user experience, and brand identity. This includes having a visually appealing brand, creating an enjoyable user experience, and maintaining a cohesive, professional aesthetic.

Exercise 9f

Note how you address the need for aesthetics.

Self-Actualisation (Fulfilling Potential)

If you sell to people

Self-actualisation represents the pinnacle of personal growth - realising one's talents, purpose, and potential. It's about becoming the best version of oneself, whether through creativity, leadership, or personal achievement.

If you sell to organisations

The equivalent is purpose-driven growth and industry leadership. At this stage, a business focuses on its mission and vision, inspiring others, setting new standards, and making a meaningful impact in its field.

Exercise 9g

Note how you address the need for fulfilling one's potential.

Transcendence (Beyond the Self)

If you sell to people

At the highest level, individuals focus on helping others reach their potential. This could involve altruism, spiritual enlightenment, or making contributions that benefit humanity. Transcendence represents the ultimate expression of connection and purpose.

If you sell to organisations

The equivalent is corporate social responsibility, mentorship, and legacy. Beyond self-actualisation, businesses can seek to support their community, give back, and create opportunities for others to succeed.

Exercise 9h

Note how you address the needs to help others and do things beyond oneself.

Your Needs Analysis Summary

If you wish, you can consolidate the results of your needs analysis to this page.

Your Audience

Your Audience

Your Audience

Exercise 10

What can you say, guess or assume about your audience? Use the text below to prompt you (and please don't feel constrained by the categories or prompts).

Demographics

What is their likely age range (e.g. children, teens, young adults, middle-aged, seniors)? Are they predominantly male or female? What is their educational background (e.g. high school, college, graduate degree)? What is their marital status (e.g. single, partnered, married, divorced)? Do they have children or dependents?

Socioeconomics

What is their income level (e.g. low, middle, high)? Do they have disposable income for non-essential products or services? What is their occupation or profession? Are they likely to be homeowners or renters? Are they located in urban, suburban, semi-rural or rural areas? What is their employment status (e.g. employed, self-employed, unemployed, retired)?

Cultural and Social

Factors: What languages do they speak? What religions or belief systems might influence their behaviour? What are their likely cultural traditions or customs? What is their ethnic background or heritage? Are they part of any social communities or networks?

Psychographics

What are their hobbies, interests, or passions? What are their values (e.g. sustainability, health, family)? Are they risk-takers or risk-averse? Do they prioritise quality over price, or vice versa? What kind of lifestyle do they lead (e.g. active, sedentary, adventurous)?

Behavioural Factors

What are their buying habits (e.g. frequent shoppers, bargain hunters, brand loyalists)? Are they innovators, early adopters, mainstream buyers, or laggards when it comes to new products? Are they likely to respond to promotions, discounts, or loyalty programmes? How do they consume information (e.g. social media, TV, newspapers, blogs)?

Needs and Challenges

Are they seeking convenience, affordability, prestige, or innovation? Do they require special features or accommodations?

Digital Presence and Technology Use

Are they tech-savvy or prefer traditional methods? Which social media platforms do they use? Are they likely to own and use smartphones, tablets, or desktops? Do they prefer mobile apps, websites, or physical stores? Are they likely to engage with brands through email, social media, or SMS?

Geographic and Environmental Factors

Where do they live? Are they affected by their local climate (e.g. hot, cold, rainy), or by climate change? Do they live in areas with certain transportation options (e.g. public transport, cars), or limitations? Are they influenced by regional trends or norms? How does the local economy or cost of living impact their decisions?

Aspirations and Motivations

What are their personal goals (e.g. career success, fitness, financial stability)? Are they likely motivated by status, security, or self-improvement? Are they drawn to products or services that offer luxury, exclusivity, or practicality? How important is brand alignment with their personal identity? Do they seek out products that help them save time or effort?

Relational and Social Dynamics

Are they influenced by family or friends in their purchasing decisions? Are they members of any organisations, clubs, or professional groups? How important is their community or social standing? Do they seek products or services that foster connection or individuality?

Some Useful Theory

Our Brain

This is to give you some background to some principles we have touched on already, and which we will mention more of later.

Earlier we said we would use *Attention, Interest, Desire, and Action* (AIDA) as the model for our prospect's cognitive journey. If we are going to take these people on a cognitive trip, it's a good idea to know how to talk to the parts of the bran we are activating.

Paul MacLean[2] divided the human brain into three parts, The Triune Model. He suggested they reflect three different evolutionary layers.

The Reptilian Brain

This is the oldest part of the brain, sometimes called the brainstem. Its function is to control basic survival functions like heartbeat, breathing and instincts. It's responsible for behaviours essential to staying alive, such as fight, flight, or freeze responses. Its characteristics are automatic, rigid and reactive - focussed solely on survival. Everything gets processed here first before it moves on.

Clearly we need to address this part of the brain when we are looking to get attention. It might also be deployed at the moment of taking action. 'Must have' responses can involve the Reptilian Brain.

The Mammalian Brain

... or the emotional brain, is often referred to as the limbic system. Its function is to manage emotions, memory, and social bonding. This part helps us to recognise and respond to feelings like fear, pleasure, and love. It also influences our relationships and sense of attachment. Its characteristics are emotional, nurturing, and focused on connection and security.

We can appeal to this part of the brain when we are looking to get attention by using familiar and comfortable images. We can also address it when creating desire.

'Would like to have' and 'Should have' responses may involve the Mammalian Brain.

The Human Brain

This is the thinking brain and is referred to as the neocortex, which is the most advanced part of the brain. Its function is to handle reasoning, planning, language, creativity, and self-awareness. It allows for abstract thinking, problem solving, and making deliberate decisions. Its characteristics are rational, reflective, and imaginative - focused on long-term goals and higher-order thinking. This thinking takes effort.

We need to satisfy the Human Brain when generating interest and desire. 'Should have' and 'Could have' responses may involve the Human Brain.

In Summary

If we tried to argue the case for the triune model with neuroscientists we may not get very far, because science found it interesting for a while and then moved on. It's too simplistic for their purposes.

However, it's very useful for ours.

Here's a simple key. If the sort of thing you are presenting would make a cave man point at it and grunt, then you have activated the Reptilian Brain. Think *tool, food, sex,* and so on.

If it's rational and analytical, then you've activated the Human Brain.

Anything else, especially if feelings are involved, then you've activated the Mammalian Brain.

In our marketing, it makes sense to address the right kind of brain at the right time, and talk to it in its language.

Fast and Slow Thinking

Here's another very useful model. *Fast and Slow Thinking* is from the work of Daniel Kahneman[3]. With just two layers, it's even simpler than the three-layer model.

Now that I've said his two-layer model is *"even simpler"*, I need to let you know he got a Nobel Prize for his work. There's a lot to it, as you'll learn if you read his book *Thinking, Fast and Slow*.

He describes two modes of thinking which you'll probably be able to relate to. You're hopefully using *slow thinking* right now because you are reading this and devoting energy to it. When you brushed your teeth this morning, or were pouring your corn flakes, you were probably using *fast thinking*.

Fast Thinking

Fast Thinking is automatic, intuitive, and almost effortless. It operates quickly and is driven by instincts, learned patterns, and emotional responses. This mode of thinking allows us to make rapid decisions in everyday situations, such as recognising faces, understanding simple sentences, or reacting to immediate dangers.

While *fast thinking* is efficient and essential for survival, it is also prone to biases and errors, as it relies on simple and convenient thinking packages (heuristics), and shortcuts, rather than deliberate analysis.

Slow Thinking

Slow Thinking on the other hand is deliberate, analytical, and effortful. This mode engages when tasks require careful consideration, such as solving complex problems, making logical arguments, or planning long-term strategies. It demands focus and often consumes more mental resources, making it slower than its counterpart.

Slow thinking is more accurate and reliable, as it critically evaluates information and resists impulsive conclusions, but it can be tiring and is less frequently activated in daily life, unless explicitly required.

An Analogy

If you need an analogy, then let's use one from the kitchen.

The difference between the two modes can be likened to the difference between heating up a microwave meal and creating a dinner from fresh ingredients.

One is good for survival. It's prepackaged (that's your analogy for a 'heuristic' right there), quick and convenient, and great for when you are in a hurry. You have eaten the same meal many times before because it gets you through the day, but the chances are you will forget this one too, just like all the others.

The home cooked dinner takes more effort and time, but the results are calculated, desired, and the outcomes unique and more memorable. While the effort produces lovely results, it's harder to keep up this sort of effort for every meal.

An Example

Let's imagine you are driving down a very familiar road which is clear of traffic, and your favourite song is on the radio, which you are enthusiastically singing along to as you know the words. We might conclude you are in Fast Thinking mode. That's because so much is familiar and automatic.

How do we know that? Well, there's a very busy junction at the end of this section of the road. There are no traffic lights to help, and you'll need to cross over. Only when there is a suitable gap in both directions, will you be able to drive across. The road bears away out of view on each side and it's an accident black spot.

Traffic is often speeding past. It takes skill to judge a gap when it's safe to go.

Take a moment or two to imagine yourself stopped at the junction, and looking up and down the road. Take note of the sights and sounds, and the feel of the steering wheel in your hands. In particular, note what you are doing.

Have you done that?

Here's a question. In your image of yourself sitting there waiting to drive across the junction, were you still happily singing along to the radio?

If you were not, then you were also re-living what slow thinking is like.

That Slow Thinking level of concentration takes a lot of energy and is hard to sustain. But it is useful, to say the least, to be able to do it when we need to.

Application

When we prepare our marketing and using *AIDA*, or when we are selling, we should be aware of how our prospects are transitioning between these thinking styles.

It might be safe to assume that before we have their attention, they are in Fast Thinking mode, and that our attention-grabbing hooks need to appeal to them in that 'language'.

And then when we have caught their attention, we might need to get them into Slow Thinking. Perhaps they won't buy unless we have slowed their thinking down so they can perceive and process the detail, and appreciate the compelling reasons why they should become a customer.

But what happens when we ask the prospect for the order, or we want them to take action? Do you want your customer to revert to Fast Thinking again?

So much depends upon the context of the situation. Looking at different scenarios suggest that either is possible. Compare a complex engineering sale where negotiations may have been ongoing for weeks, to the impulse purchase of a dinner set from a trader at a market stall.

We'll look at this in a little more detail in the *Sales Bootcamp* later. It's a very interesting subject and one you may like to explore independently.

But for now, just be aware of the two modes.

Attention

Attention-Grabbing Hooks

Exercise 11

Let's look at the first stage of AIDA. For each of the three layers of the brain, design one or more attention-grabbing hooks for your offering.

Reptilian:

This brain layer reacts to threats, safety, and basic needs like food, sex, and dominance. Make it primal. Use food imagery, face and eye contact, fear, urgency, sensory contrast, or dominance to trigger a strong instinctual response.

Example: *"WARNING: This Common Mistake Could Be Costing You Thousands!"*

Mammalian:

This brain system responds to emotions, relationships, and tribal belonging. Make it feel personal. Use storytelling and personal narratives, social proof, cute and nurturing stimuli, songs that evoke nostalgia, and controversy that stir values.

Example: *"I Quit My 9-to-5 and Built a Dream Business – Here's How."*

Human:

This brain layer is responsible for problem-solving, abstract thinking, and learning. Make it intriguing by using curiosity gaps, puzzles, or new ideas to engage the rational mind.

Example: *"Why Do Some Businesses Succeed While Others Fail? The Answer May Surprise You."*

Getting Attention

To get attention, what we present has to be easily understood at a glance. *Fast Thinking* has to be able to decode it. The lower down the three-layer brain model we appeal to, the better our chances of getting attention. This is why images of people looking at you work very well, but a block of dense text won't.

It should also stand out visually. This means it should contrast with everything around it. We'd notice someone if they were wearing a white hat in a room where others are wearing black ones, or if they were the only one jumping up and down.

It doesn't have to just contrast visually. Any change for the senses can be used. A sudden noise or a change of texture can grab our attention too.

This is because our brains are *prediction engines*. They are always predicting what to expect in the next moment, based on the moments that have just passed. When it perceives something that it did not expect, it devotes attention to it. We should bear this in mind when trying to get attention.

You can use text to grab attention, but what you say has to be short and challenging. *Fast Thinking* can decode punchy statements. To do this, you can ask a question, or say something that challenges a comfortable assumption, or bias.

A poster is an example of something that needs to get attention if it is to work.

On the next page, you'll see a poster. It is divided into five elements. At least one of those elements is there to get attention. We are not just focussing on attention right now; we're also looking at the poster structure too. You might want to use a structure like this for a web page or a leaflet, for instance.

These are not rules, more a suggested template for when you need one. These are the five elements that the poster uses.

1. The *situation before*. It uses an image to do this.
2. It *challenges* an assumption with a punchy statement or asks a challenging question. For example, you could say "98% of people won't help Jane."
3. It *tells a story*. It might be punchy text, an image, or it might be a longer read.
4. It has a *call to action* - a CTA. This can be an instruction, a QR code for more information, or anything else action oriented. For example, it could be: "Save a life today and give blood."
5. The *happy day scenario*. In other words, the 'after state' which compares favourably to the 'before state'.

It's possible to reduce the number of elements if, for instance, your company name is the CTA: *buymeacoffee.com* would be an example.

Or if it is part of the story, like: *webuyanycar.com*.

You can also make the happy day scenario the story.

This five-part structure addresses all of *AIDA* of course, not just *Attention*.

Exercise 12a

In a moment, you'll sketch out your own poster. Before you do, take a moment to work out the *AIDA* steps addressed by each element of this poster.

Exercise 12b

Now it's your turn. Sketch a poster for your business. Include: 1. a 'before' state, 2. a challenging hook, 3. a story, 4. a CTA, and 5. a happy day scenario.

Interest

Your Value Proposition

We are using the *AIDA* framework as the backbone of your investigation. Now, let's focus on: *Interest*.

To help you effectively address this in one step, we'll use a value proposition template inspired by Geoffrey Moore[4] in his book: *Crossing the Chasm*.

This template is a powerful tool for clarifying the unique value your product or service offers. By working through it, you can structure your ideas to highlight your understanding of your customers' needs while demonstrating how your offering stands out from the competition. Here's an example for Patagonia:

"For outdoor enthusiasts who value sustainability and high performance, Patagonia is an outdoor apparel brand that provides durable, eco-friendly clothing. Unlike fast fashion retailers, our solution prioritises ethical sourcing and environmental responsibility, empowering customers to make choices that align with their values."

Here's the template. There are seven variables:

For (your audience) who (statement of need or opportunity), (your product or service name) is a (product/service category) that (statement of benefit). Unlike (primary competitive alternative), our solution (statement of differentiation).

When it comes to articulating competitive alternatives, you don't necessarily need to think about a company. What the customers *use or do today* can be the competition.

Exercise 13

Now it's your turn. Use what you have worked out about your audience, their needs, their hot buttons, and your benefits, to write your value proposition.

Desire

Four Questions

The third step in your prospect's cognitive *AIDA* journey is *Desire* - arguably the most powerful and nuanced element. If you've ever watched *Mad Men*[5], you'll know what a monumental subject this is, especially for consumer products.

Let's start by making sure that four generic pre-requisites are met. We'll look at the more subjective side of desire in a later worksheet, but here, we are going to make sure there's nothing to stop your prospect generating desire.

There are four unspoken, and possibly subconscious, questions in your prospect's mind. Consider them show-stoppers if not addressed properly. The good news is this structure is super-useful in a wide variety of situations, and you already have responses for three of them. We'll get responses for the fourth next. These are the questions.

Do I trust you?

This question is about the subjective connection between you and your prospect. Trust is rooted in their confidence that: you understand their needs, you are experienced and knowledgeable, and you will support them if things go wrong. You can demonstrate trustworthiness through actions like displaying industry association logos, customer testimonials, or awards wherever your brand appears. Your Trust Framework (Exercise 3) informs this question.

Is this good for me?

This question is deeply personal and taps into your prospect's relationship with your offering. They might be thinking, how will this improve my reputation, status, or relationships? Or: will it make me feel accomplished, happy, or secure? Your prospect's emotional hot buttons that you address are critical here (Exercise 7).

Do I understand?

This is a logical layer. Your prospect needs to feel that your product or service makes sense in their unique context. Does it address their specific pain points? Does it provide lasting value? What are the risks, and can they manage them? The features and benefits of your offering are the foundations for this. (Exercise 4 and 7)

Does it work?

This is your opportunity to prove your offering's effectiveness. Whether through tailored demonstrations, detailed case studies, testimonials or just beautiful presentation, your prospect needs evidence that your product or service works as promised. We'll look at this next.

Deploying these questions

These four questions form a very useful structure that you can apply to any communication to ensure it is complete, such as your website, leaflet, presentations, and conversations.

We can separate these four in two ways. Notice that the first two are more subjective than the last two, which are more objective. Also notice that an alternative pair deals with things external to the prospect (you and your offering) while the remaining questions are concerned with things that are more internal.

It's important to note that you should remain open-minded about the order you present these in. Each one is an entry point for different kinds of people. An engineer might need to understand technicalities first, and make sure it works before considering it as a solution. A business owner on the other hand may seek your credibility first, and ask, *"Do I trust you?"* Their next enquiry could be, *"How is this good for my business?"* Being open-minded is the key.

Does it work?

As mentioned, you already have assets to answer three of the questions. We are left with *Does it work?* to be thought about.

Your customers won't want to take your word for this. They will either want to see things work with their own eyes, in which case, the nature of your business will define how you demonstrate your offering, or they may take other people's word for it. This can be in the form of case studies, accolades, reviews, and research papers. *Social proof* is a very powerful method, and we will talk more about that later.

If it helps, you might want to apply the three-part model of the human brain to structure your thoughts here. This is best illustrated though an example - a client who bakes, and sells, cakes on a market stall.

Reptilian

She makes a point of cutting a slice out of a new cake so that customers can see inside. This visual treat appeals to the reptilian brain.

Mammalian

Many of her customers are senior men. They appreciate the idea of taking home some home-made comforts like the ones their wives, mothers and grandmothers used to make.

Making traditional cakes reminds them of their past family life.

Human

Working out how to get cake home in one piece requires suitable packaging. Displaying a pre-packaged portion answers any questions about this that the human mind may be concerned with.

Exercise 14

Now it's your turn. Decide how you will answer the question 'Does it work?'

56

The 'Ick Factor'

The purpose of your marketing is to build trust, desire, and curiosity. Let's look at something you should specifically avoid.

In marketing, the 'Ick Factor' refers to a negative emotional reaction your audience has to something you present. It can be anything that crosses an invisible line where the prospect says, *"No, it's just not for me."*

It might involve a mild feeling of unease or discomfort, all the way to weapons-grade disgust. Let's just agree for now that *anything* that might move the needle on an ick-o-meter should be avoided.

'Ick' is a gut reaction that stems from the Mammalian Brain. We have an instinctive aversion to things that feel unsafe, unclean, doesn't align with our values or offends our morals. This aversion will probably override any rational interest the Human Brain may have in your offering. *Fast Thinking* will make your prospect's mind up for them.

Typical things that can turn people away are provocative statements, inconsistency, anything fake, edgy, creepy or cringe-worthy, over-sharing, being over-salesy ... the list goes on and on. Let's take a very mild case.

Say someone sets up a café that is a strong reflection of their personality, and they do it in a market town. They like sweet things, and have used light and pastel colours, and images of cakes and flowers in the décor. They have a wide variety of cakes on display, where thick layers of cream predominate. But the café is always empty. There's nothing wrong with the venue - people may visit it to buy cakes to take home - it's just that they don't use it as a café, which is how it is branded.

What makes people think, *"It's just not for me?"* There may be more than one Ick Factor at play.

We'll start with roughly half the population. Most males may not be able to see themselves relaxing in such a pristine environment, especially when there are other, more 'down to earth' venues nearby.

The second is the expectation that people should identify with a public display of over-indulgence. This will be at odds with how many people view themselves: as independent, and with a healthy lifestyle.

The problem for us is that our audience probably won't tell us when they get the 'ick'. They'll just vote with their feet, and we'll have a void where we were expecting something to happen.

Ick factors can infiltrate our best efforts at any time, and I can only sensitise you to the subject so you can be on your guard.

When we look at *Liking and Alikeness*, we'll explore safe and positive areas to navigate your marketing towards, but for now, let's investigate one potential source of 'ick' in your business.

Yes. I'm talking about you. For better or worse, business owners leak their personal traits into their business and brand. Some can of course give the business character and make it memorable for the right reasons, but for others it can be wrong.

If you choose to proceed with the next worksheet, you'll first explore your own experience of ick as part of sensitisation. You'll then look at your quirks to check that you aren't doing a disservice to your business by leaking too much about you into your brand, taking the spotlight away from your audience's needs.

I'm going to drop the solution now and leave it with you, so you'll know what the remedy is. If this is 'a thing', then what's needed is an honest willingness to tone down a trait, even if it is important to you. I'll leave that there for you to put in place if needed.

Are you ready to 'face the cringe'? Let's go!

Exercise 15

Take a moment and recall at least five situations when you thought that something, or someone, made you feel 'ick'.

Can you think about what it was that made you feel 'ick'. If you wish, you could complete this sentence for each one.

"It was not for me because ..."

Column 3

Don't filter: write down at least six quirks about yourself - your personality, habits, beliefs, or style - that you bring to the business. Say at least 3 each of the strongest things you are proud of, and not proud of.

Column 4

Put yourself in the shoes of an important prospect who is quietly interested in buying from you in bulk. Dial each quirk up to the max. What is the impact of each one?

Scenarios

Desire will be strongest when your prospect envisions themself using your product or service - and feels the emotions that come with it. You can only do yourself favours by being aware of those moments.

To help you log these important connections, you'll create short scripts for significant moments that you think your customer will experience when benefitting from your offering. Include those moments of anticipation too, and of reflection afterwards. You'll describe the moment, and then what they *think* and *feel*.

So, 'what's the relationship between these scenarios and the hot buttons?' you might ask. Hot buttons are about an emotional reaction to a feature after all.

Well, these are based on events for a start, and then we've added thoughts and feelings. You can't make a video short for a hot button, but you can from these. The information is richer. They could ably inform the specific photos or imagery you need to connect with your audience.

Here are three examples for a supper club. The page is split into two parts.

Moment / Scenario	Thoughts and Feelings
A young woman puts on her makeup in preparation for a supper club event.	*She's looking forward to the event, wondering who she will meet, and hoping she'll be noticed and fit in.*
As she approaches the venue, she can see people talking and laughing inside.	*She feels excited about meeting someone who she finds interesting and who finds her interesting too.*
As she approaches the door, the organiser-host welcomes her warmly and checks her in.	*She's relieved that she's in the right place, that everything is well organised and that she won't be on her own for long.*

Now it's your turn!

On the next page, identify the scenarios where your customer *is happier* in some way because:

- they are going to use,
- are using,
- or have used your offering.

For each one, say what you can about that moment, and what they are seeing, hearing, and experiencing. In the second column, describe their feelings and positive thoughts.

Exercise 16

Moment / Scenario	*Thoughts and Feelings*

Action

Action

Introduction

We arrive at the last part of *AIDA* which is *Action*.

In a relatively simple situation like a web page, the action we want the user to take could be to press a button that has some imperative on it like: *'Click here'*. The button could simply reveal the answer to an FAQ question or do lots more, like purchase an item. In either case, we still need to make sure the previous three AIDA steps are intact, or else the user won't press the button.

The most complicated situation where *action* is initiated is when selling face-to-face. As a business owner, you wear a lot of hats, and *Sales* is one of them. There's a lot involved in that moment when a prospect actually makes up their mind to buy your product or service. A lot goes into the lead-up too. In fact, when selling from cold, a salesman will start with *getting attention* and then work towards the *close* which is another word for the customer taking *action*. They follow *AIDA*, but they use their own language.

(I'm going to say it. A lot of sales language give me the 'ick'. It feels sociopathic to me but I'm going to stick with convention.)

We are going to look at selling - it's the most complicated, teased-out and organic version of the *action* step available. Here's why.

- It has its own activities.
- If you get it right for face-to-face situations, you'll be better equipped to generate action in your marketing. It might help your website design to be more effective, for example. Or it will make sure you have an effective CTA on a leaflet.
- You may have had no training in sales; in which case the following pages may be a useful entry point. Welcome to *Structured Selling*.

So far, we have taken a customer-centric approach and mostly thought about marketing.

Marketing is a remote process, but selling is personal; it's conducted face-to-face, or over the phone. Selling also includes controls to protect your commercial interests. I'd like to explain that.

When I introduced AIDA, I used the analogy of a couple of trains, *Interest* and *Desire*, that depart their station when the *Attention* whistle was blown. Now consider a third train, *Sales*. It's used for maintenance, and it runs on its own dedicated track that passes through each station and runs parallel to the other lines. When selling, you are on this train.

The first thing we do on the Sales Track is *qualify* your prospect to make sure a sale is possible. Then during the journey, you regularly check that *Interest* and *Desire* are still moving towards the destination. Each check is called a *Trial Close*.

When *Interest* and *Desire* arrive at their destination, we arrive at a critical moment. The role of *Sales* is to *ask for the order* and that process is called *Closing*. When the customer gives you the order, that's the *Action* we were looking for. As mentioned, we can imagine a flash going off at that point. (Somebody obviously tipped off the press.)

However, sometimes, one of the prospect's trains may not quite reach the destination, but it can appear as though it has. The prospect has an *objection* of some sort, and we need to find out what it is. The sales train carries a special technique for eventualities like this, and it's called *objection handling*.

What follows is a very short sales boot camp where we look at these ideas and practice a few core techniques. Practice is important because it helps you say the right thing in the heat of the moment.

Sales Boot Camp - Qualification

Selling face-to-face brings special challenges. People are not rational animals. Selling can be a dark art practiced in unpredictable circumstances, so it should be no surprise that salespeople use techniques to make things more predictable. Whether you have a market stall or are selling complex software, you are still dealing with the Mk 1 Human Being, so the same rules apply to all cases.

Qualification is the process of determining whether a prospect is a good fit for your product or service, and they have the resources to pay. Your purpose is to save time and effort by focusing only on people that are likely to *convert*.

Qualification can be achieved by asking a question like *"Do you have some cake to enjoy with your tea later?"* or *"Are you in a position to make a decision today?"*

If the prospect's circumstances are more complicated, you can be more specific: *"Are you in a position to decide today, or should we bring someone else into the conversation?"*

BANT is a structure that stands for Budget, Authority, Need and Timeline. It covers these questions:

- Can they afford to buy it?
- Do they have the authority to buy?
- Do they have a need or potential desire for your offering?
- Is the timing right?

Exercise 17

It's your turn. Given what you know about your offering, and your audience, what could you ask your prospect to qualify them early on?

Sales Boot Camp - Trial Close

This is the golden thread you weave into the fabric of AIDA. More specifically, you do this intermittently while you are creating *Interest* and *Desire*. The purpose is to check in with your prospect to see how they think or feel about your proposal as you proceed, and you should do it in a way that is comfortable for both parties.

Typically, this is undertaken by asking simple questions, and ideally ones where the answer can't wrong-foot you. In effect, you are gauging a prospect's readiness to buy before making a full commitment. It helps to uncover any potential objections early on and you might do this by asking a simple: *How does that sound so far.*

Here are some other examples:

- *Can you see this sofa in your living room?*
- *Can you see your staff using this app?*

When we look at influence and getting commitment later, you'll see there's a lot of overlap to explore there. Getting a series of small incremental agreements improves our chances of success when we ask for the order.

Exercise 18a

What sort of questions could you ask along the way to either get agreement, or to check if there are any objections you will need to address?

Exercise 18b

What could you say in response to an answer that isn't what you expected?

Sales Boot Camp - Closing

Closing is about *asking for the order*. Closing is a *Call to Action* that wears sunglasses and rides a motorbike. Seriously though, if we don't ask, we don't get. We need to get used to *asking for the order*.

For us, this is the final step in the sales process where the sale is formally agreed upon and the prospect becomes a customer. In sales parlance, they *convert*. *Closing* as a term gives me the 'ick' as mentioned, but there's absolutely nothing stopping you making a warm and joyous experience of it.

When the path to closing is a natural and smooth one, closing itself might be no big deal. Almost unnoticeable. However, we are dealing with human beings here, who might still engage the fight, flight or freeze response of their reptilian brain when asked to commit. This is despite you showing them how much rational sense your offering makes and how great your solution is.

Salespeople are taught techniques that move things over the line, sometimes even acting as if they already are! It can be like watching a hypnotist at work. Here are some closing techniques and examples.

Spot the ones where an assumptive close is also used.

· Alternative: "Since your gutters are badly blocked, let's sort this out. Should we come Thursday or Friday?"

· Summary: "So, just to recap - you're getting our early-bird offer and delivery to your home. Everything seems ready. Would you like to go ahead?"

· Urgency: "As you know, this offer is available until sold out. If you want the special pricing, we'll need to move on this today. How would you like to pay?"

· Testimonial: "I bought a pair of those myself. Shall I box them up for you?"

It's super-super-important to **keep quiet** once you have asked for the order. It's tempting, but do not interrupt the prospect while they think and get used to the idea of becoming a customer.

Exercise 19

Now it's your turn. Imagine yourself at the point when it's time to ask for the order. What might you say that sounds natural for you and your business? Be sure to imagine yourself keeping quiet until your prospect speaks, no matter how awkward.

Sales Boot Camp - Handling Objections

An objection is a concern, doubt, or barrier raised by a prospect that prevents them from committing to a purchase. Treat objections like a natural part of the sales process. At the very least, they can signal that your prospect is engaged and considering your offer. You might hear:

- *I want to think about it.*
- *I'm happy with what I've got.*
- *I'll have to talk to someone.*
- *I don't have the budget right now.*
- *I don't need this.*

When we hear an objection, we naturally hear a showstopper. At face value, they seem like a rejection. However, remember that it's easier for us humans to dismiss a whole offer when we have an issue about a detail, even though we may be in favour generally.

Handling objections effectively involves understanding the prospect's concerns and addressing them empathetically. Here's a structure:

- listen
- empathise
- respond and
- get confirmation that the issue has been resolved.

So, when you hear a prospect say, *"I want to think about it."* you might respond with something like:

"Sure. When people say they want to think about it, it usually means they are unsure about certain things. Wouldn't you agree? (Wait for the answer). Can we look at those things?"

Exercise 20

Now it's your turn. For these objections, think of a response that you could make.

Objection	*Your Response*

I'm happy with what I've got.

I'll have to talk to someone first.

It's a bit pricey.

I don't need this.

Influence

The Six Principles of Influence

Let's cover some super-useful techniques.

We'll start with The Six Principles of Influence. This is a valuable framework from Robert Cialdini[6], and it's considered an early example of nudge theory. Nudge theory is concerned with small changes that can have a disproportionate effect, and it's a very interesting subject that's well worth researching.

His six principles provide a framework for understanding how to persuade and motivate people effectively. Each principle taps into human psychology, making them powerful tools for influencing behaviour.

Those principles are:

- Reciprocity
- Commitment and Consistency
- Social Proof
- Authority
- Liking
- Scarcity

Many of these seem blindingly obvious and you'll recognise when you have been exposed to them in the past. But there's a lot to this. It's really useful that these principles have been brought together in one package.

We will take each one in turn. Each principle comes with a short explanation, after which you are provided with space to make notes on how you might apply the principle in your marketing and sales.

Reciprocity

In the 'Coca-Cola experiment' by Regan[7] (1971), participants who received a small, unsolicited gift (a soft drink) from a researcher were more likely to purchase raffle tickets from them later, even if the tickets cost more than the drink. This demonstrates how small acts of generosity can create a sense of obligation.

People feel compelled to return favours or kindness, even if they did not request them.

This principle stems from a universal social norm that values mutual exchange, which is activated when we start giving.

Typically, a business will look to offer things that cost them little but have value for their audience. Examples may be: free samples, downloadable guides, or an introductory consultation.

Exercise 21

What could you offer your audience that would be low-cost for you, but would be valuable to your audience?

Your offer

And what could you ask for in return?

Commitment and Consistency

The "foot-in-the-door" experiment by Freedman and Fraser[8] (1966) asked participants to put a small sign in their window promoting safe driving. Later, they were asked to display a large, unsightly billboard with the same message in their garden. Those who agreed to the small, initial request were significantly more likely to agree to the larger request, showing the power of incremental commitments.

Once people commit to something, they strive to act in ways that are consistent with their previous commitments. Public commitments are especially powerful, as individuals wish to appear consistent to others.

Salespeople might regularly ask their prospect if they agree so far. Getting a series of small 'yes' agreements make it harder for the prospect to say 'no' later when asked for the order.

Exercise 22

Think of some small 'asks' you could make of your audience and then identify what action the prospect might be asked to take later.

Small asks

Future action requested

71

Social Proof

In an experiment by Milgram, Bickman, and Berkowitz[9] (1969), researchers had individuals stand on a busy New York City street and look up at a building. When a single person looked up, few passers-by followed suit, but as the group size increased, a much larger percentage of people copied the behaviour. This highlighted the role of social proof in guiding behaviour.

People are influenced by the actions and behaviours of others, especially in uncertain situations. They look to others to determine what is correct or appropriate.

For instance, restaurants use this by allowing a queue to form outside, even though there are spaces available inside. They will also seed tip jars with money, so customers can feel comfortable joining in.

Posting online gives many opportunities to present social proof. Case studies, reviews, videos, and images can give a sense of others using your offering. But there are other ways to show that people use you, especially if you provide your service to their home. For instance, putting personalised postcards through the doors of the neighbours of your latest customer may seem old-school, but it can be highly effective.

Exercise 23

What authentic evidence can you present that would demonstrate other people use your product or service?

Authority

Milgram's obedience experiment[10] (1963) revealed the powerful influence of authority figures. Participants were instructed by an experimenter in a lab coat to administer electric shocks to a "learner". Despite their discomfort, many participants complied, even administering shocks they believed to be harmful, simply because the instruction came from an authority figure.

People are more likely to comply with requests or follow guidance from individuals who appear to have authority or expertise. A simple example would be the success of the George Foreman Grill, which sold over 100 million units once George Foreman's name was put on it.

Using authority does not have to mean someone in authority endorses you. It can be acquired through association; through the network you associate or collaborate with. Another approach is to engage in thought leadership, the production of white papers or research.

Here are some questions to prompt your thoughts:

- Who do you know, who's opinion matters, who might say something about you?
- Which people or organisations would be suitable for you to be associated with?
- Who can you publicly collaborate with in some way?
- How can you demonstrate your authority? It could be in a domain unrelated to your business.

Exercise 24

How can you associate with authority to influence prospects to have faith in you and your company?

Likability and Alikeness

This is the antidote to *ick factors*.

In a study by Emswiller, Deaux, and Willits[11] (1971), participants were more likely to comply with a request for money when the requester was dressed similarly to them, highlighting how similarity fosters liking and increases compliance.

People are more inclined to say "yes" to those they like, or who are like them. Factors such as physical attractiveness, similarity, compliments, group membership and familiarity can all increase likeability. People are drawn to those who dress similarly or reflect a style they admire. Shared appearance can evoke a sense of "belonging" or relatability. They also like those who "speak their language", whether it's using industry jargon, humour, or cultural references.

Exercise 25

What can you do overtly to promote liking and alikeness? Exercise 10 was about the attributes of your audience. Use that to prompt you.

Scarcity

Worchel, Lee, and Adewole[12] (1975) conducted a study in the U.S. where participants were shown jars of cookies containing either ten or two items and asked to try one and rate it for desirability. Separately, some subjects were shown a jar of ten from which eight were removed in front of them. Subjects rated the cookies differently, the lowest being the jar of ten, the highest being the jar that was reduced to two in front of the subject, even though the items were identical. This demonstrated how scarcity increases perceived value.

People perceive opportunities or items as more valuable when they are scarce or limited. Scarcity generates a sense of urgency and fear of missing out (FOMO).

Here are some examples:

- Time-based scarcity, including early bird discounts, flash sales and future price rises.
- Quantity-based scarcity, including bin ends, and visible stock counts.
- Deliberate rarity including limiting production runs and serial numbering.
- Exclusive access, including VIP rewards and hidden sales.

Exercise 26

How might you use scarcity to motivate your audience?

Uniqueness

So, Tell Me What You Do

When we are asked, we need to be able to say what we do in a way that your listener will understand and remember. Company owners sometimes struggle to explain what they do in terms that others can understand, and that's because they know *everything* about the company. What sort of filter should they use so it makes sense to someone who knows nothing about what they do?

Making it so that another person gets what you do in one sentence can be a challenge. Oddly enough, we shouldn't talk about ourselves. We should say what we do for others instead.

This technique starts with the easily remembered expression:

"We help people to ..."

Here are some examples:

- We help people to avoid expensive repairs by clearing their gutters on a regular basis.
- We help people to grow their businesses by delivering effective digital marketing strategies.
- We help people to protect their loved ones by providing reliable home security systems.

You don't have to use this exact form of words, of course. Here's an example noticed on a van.

We decorate your new house so you can move into a new home.

Notice that the expressions deal with the time when the customer is *at their happiest* with the service or product. That is not a coincidence. Emotion and memory are linked, which is why this form of words will help people to remember you, and what you do.

Exercise 27

Now it's your turn. Work out the moment when your customers will be the happiest with your offering and create a statement around it. Something like this:

We help people to (key benefit) by (what you do for them).

Become Remarkable

When we overlap two incongruent ideas, what happens at the intersection becomes potentially remarkable. Literally. I mean people are much more likely to make a comment about it because there's something to say.

Here are some examples to demonstrate the principle.

- A restaurant where the staff sing.
- A regular 'steak night' in a pub where only an even number of steaks can be ordered.
- An IT company that only employs developers who are on the autism spectrum.
- A lawyer who used to be a ship's captain.
- A consultancy that only employs experienced seniors.
- A female-only firm of chimney sweeps.
- A cleaning company that wears 1950's styles.
- A pub that only plays blues music.

As you see, by overlapping two ideas we get something that is more than just the simple sum of the parts. It makes a new kind of sense, and it provides people with something to say about the event, person, or company.

If you take the example of a ship's captain who studied law while sailing the oceans, his specialised knowledge makes him the go-to legal professional for maritime matters. Both subjects (being a lawyer and being a ship's captain) separately are not *remarkable*, but together they are. They'll help him to get business.

Let's see if we can intersect your business with something from your world. The thing you bring in to overlap with your business need not be startling. It can be a hobby or something you like. Such as: *the accountant who keeps fish*.

So now you now know why you were asked early on to make a list of previous jobs, hobbies, little known facts and so on, in Exercise 2.

It's time to review that list to see which one of those is most suitable to intersect with your new company to make you, or your brand, literally remarkable.

Exercise 28

Select the best attribute from Exercise 2 and use it to complete this sentence:

The [your company type] who/that [attribute phrase.

Getting Your Message Out There

Getting Your Message Out There

A Roadmap

This workbook is about DIY marketing, but for the sake of orientation we'll look at the whole picture from the top down. There are three layers to this onion.

1 Be Findable

This ensures your audience can discover and recognise your business without effort. It creates credibility and makes it easy for customers to contact you. Suggestions:

Consistent branding: logo, colours, messaging.

· Domain name: Get this early on because you will want to put it on everything. People are more likely to click a link or scan a QR code these days, than type it in, but being able to say your domain name is still important especially when it comes to your email address. Short words are good, and it's even better if you make your domain name part of your story or CTA.

- Website: At least a simple, one-pager with contact details.
- Google Business Profile / Maps listing
- Signwriting: van, shopfront, worksite boards.
- Branded apparel: for staff, or as a giveaway.
- Social media profiles: even if just a basic presence.
- Printed material: business cards, leaflets, case studies.

2 Get Noticed

Once your business is findable, the next step is to actively reach out to potential customers. These methods require time and effort but can be done with minimal costs.

Examples:

- Networking: attending local events, trade shows, business groups.
- Social media engagement: posting, commenting, direct outreach.
- Word of mouth and referrals: encouraging satisfied customers to spread the word.
- Collaborations: partnering with other businesses to cross-promote.
- Email marketing: simple newsletters or offers to previous customers.
- Cold outreach: direct messages, emails, calls to potential clients.
- Content marketing: blogging, video tutorials, social posts that educate or entertain.

3 Grow

Once your business has a foundation, paid-for marketing can help scale and attract new customers faster. The key is to spend wisely on what delivers the best return. Examples:

- Online ads: Google Ads, Facebook/Instagram ads, LinkedIn ads.
- Sponsored content: paying influencers or media for exposure.
- Print or local ads: newspapers, magazines, community boards.
- Paid partnerships: affiliate marketing, referral incentives.
- Direct mail campaigns: postcards, flyers, catalogues.
- PR campaigns: press releases, sponsored articles.
- SEO investment: hiring someone to improve website ranking.

The Rule of Three

The human mind is a pattern-recognising machine. As mentioned earlier when talking about *getting attention*, if something disturbs a pattern we have perceived, we notice it and give it attention.

It just so happens that three is the smallest number the mind needs to form a pattern.

So, there we have it. If we want our audience's minds to latch on to us, we have to make sure we are noticed three times as a minimum. In marketing speak, that's three touches. And those touches should have a difference of some sort so that our prospects' minds detect the pattern in context.

To illustrate this, I'll use the example of a local service. The principle should still apply for a digital business because the prospect is the same model of Mk 1 Human Being.

Imagine a landscape gardener who's only channel is their van with their company logo and contact details on the side. (*Channel* is marketing speak for the medium you use to get your message to your audience. All the bullet points on the previous page are channels.)

When people drive past the van, they see the same thing every time, and each time they might give it less attention because nothing changes.

Now consider another gardener who also has a branded van and puts up a board when they are working at a client's site. They wear branded apparel and make a point of visiting the village shop for coffee when in the area. They also put postcards through doors saying how they transformed a neighbour's garden and take out a short series of adverts in the parish magazine.

Each time someone in the area sees the logo in a different place, they connect the dots so to speak. The second time is a coincidence, the third time a pattern. They start to make sense of what it is they are seeing, and that sort of brain activity is more likely to start an enquiry in their mind about how they could improve their lives with this service.

So when we say The Rule of Three, we mean three or more touches through different channels.

Yes, you are right. That's not, strictly speaking, true.

We could say *three or more different touches through one channel* if we wanted. Three different adverts for three editions of a parish magazine would be an example.

I'm going to stick with the first scenario to illustrate cross-channel marketing, but you can adapt this in any way that suits you.

One-Page Marketing Plan

We are going to create a very simple marketing plan. It's on one page and has four columns.

The idea behind a one-page plan is to constrain the document creation to a limited event and then get on with the action.

Planning is good and necessary because you avoid failure and get better results than when you don't do it. You make less mistakes on your way to your objective, and you avoid expensive re-work.

Planning usually requires time unless you are going to buy an A0 sized plotter and print out Gantt charts. (Do not do that.) You can do it in a chair with a cup of coffee. Sometimes it's too comfortable and we can get lulled into thinking we are being productive while we refine things, putting off the moment when we need to transition into *doing*. We need to do enough planning, and then draw the line, and a one-page plan helps with that discipline.

In our case, 'enough' is when you have defined sufficient marketing products to the point where you believe your audience will have a good chance of receiving enough impressions to register at least three of them.

The Columns Explained

Channels

Select the channels you want to use. It might be 'website' or 'apparel' for instance. Using AI as a research tool will give you many options to choose from.

Deliverables

These are the deliverables you want in place. The things you can hit with a stick. Examples would be posters, a website, a social account, networking events and so on.

Success

These are your quality criteria, where you answer the question 'what does success look like?' These should be stated in *measurable, testable terms*.

Hopefully, you'll err towards criteria that make the product 'fit for purpose', instead of reaching for the stars in terms of quality. This is so you expend your time and resources efficiently. What is fit for purpose for one company may be too much or too little for another, so be sure to impose your judgement about what is right for you.

Actions

Finally, do a breakdown of the steps you need to take, or delegate, to deliver the product.

Example One-Page Marketing Plan

One-Page Marketing Plan

Channels	Deliverables	Success	Actions
Website	Attractive and complete website	1. Google first page 2. Visually attractive 3. 100 new visits p m	1. Write content 2. Acquire images 3. Appoint designer 4. Define search terms
Social	• Personal LinkedIn a/c • Business FB page	• Authoritative profiles • Comments left by customers on FB	• Open accounts • Write content • Family and friends check
Printed flyer	One-page flyer that introduces us, to put through doors.	• 100 leaflets delivered by hand every week • 5 enquiries a week	1. Write content 2. Commission design 3. Send to printers 4. Schedule drops 5. Enlist volunteers
PR	Local press coverage	One article every month in the local paper	• Take more images at work • Write 3 x human interest stories • Submit 1st ones to paper

Exercise 29

Now it's your turn. Turn over to create your own plan.

Your One-Page Marketing Plan

Channels	Deliverables

Success

Actions

Optimisation

If you chose to do paid-for marketing, you'll want to manage things to get the best return on the money you spend. Here's a list of things you might want to measure for each campaign:

1. The money spent

2. The number of impressions

3. The number of hits

4. Purchases or conversions

5. Life-time customer value

You'll then be able to compare the time and money expended to get one customer (divide item 1 by the number of customers) with their average life-time value. Ideally, you'll find a sweet spot in your channels that works consistently.

Here's a bare-bones breakdown of the levers you can pull when designing a campaign.

Variation

Variety keeps an audience engaged but *consistency*, on the other hand, reinforces your brand. The Advertising Research Foundation suggests that two to three distinct, but related 'creatives' maximise impact, without being overwhelming.

Frequency

Our beliefs can be shaped by something as simple as repetition - often without us even noticing. Repeated exposure to a message can make its claims seem truer despite what we originally thought.

Frequency is about the total number of times someone receives your message across all channels before they act. For adverts, the classic 'Rule of Seven' is a starting point. However, modern data suggests anything upward of three impressions can work, and that *fatigue* properly sets in after ten.

Interval

The interval between exposures to your message should be tuned. Make it too short and you annoy people. Make it too long and you reduce recall. Intervals can be in minutes to months, and should be a match for your channel, audience, and objectives.

Channel mix

A good multi-channel approach increases reach and reinforces messaging through context. According to reports, pairing social media (which is fast and interactive) with email (which is personalised and direct) can boost effectiveness by 25-40%. That's just an example. It's important to address the same audience or you generate no overlap. We talked about this in The Rule of Three.

Personalisation

This is about how well your message aligns with specific audience groups. A generic message might need more exposure than a tailored one. Personalised ads can cut the need for exposure by 30%, (McKinsey).

Content Density

Messages can run the risk of overwhelming if they are overly complex, causing people to exit out. If complexity is required, then adverts require more exposure and slower pacing than a simple 'buy now!'.

Timing

External, real-world events can affect the receptivity of your audience to your message. External 'noise' (elections for example) can drown out ads, requiring more frequency. Perhaps there's a seasonal element to consider, or a time in the day when your audience is most receptive or available.

Exercise 30

Let's see how close you are to running a campaign.

Variations: Can you think of three distinct creative treatments, themes, or stories to use?

Frequency: How many times do you think your audience will need to hear your message before they act?

Interval: What do you think the ideal interval between exposures should be?

Audience: What is the first segment that you would like to target?

Personalisation: What specific message would you like to impart to this segment?

Channel mix: What channels would be most suitable for them?

Density: Out of ten, how dense does your content need to be?

Timing: When is the most opportune time to target your audience?

And Finally

In Closing

Our first instinct, when we start out and want to communicate about our business, is to talk about ourselves and the features of our offering. It's only to be expected. That's because it's *all we have been thinking about* for some time and it's all we know. We think; *my audience needs to know about the features and how great we are, or they won't buy, right?* I know this was true for me. It takes real effort to put yourself in your prospect's shoes and change your messages, so they become relevant.

If your recently created 'tell-us-what-you-do' sentence for Exercise 27 differs in sentiment from the slogan you wrote for Exercise 1, then you have tangible evidence of a shift in your focus.

We have spent some time looking at your audience's whole persona, in other words, the basic, the rational, and the emotional person. We spent a lot of time looking at the emotional person, and in different ways.

What have we covered? We analysed your audience's receptivity in terms of their basic needs (Maslow). There should be content in there to help you with topics you should be talking about.

We also looked at the ultimate benefits they could emotionally relate to, their hot buttons, which should help you craft hooks to get their attention. These are especially important to articulate when selling and when you demonstrate how your offering is good for them.

We covered the four areas you should articulate whenever your audience gives you their attention, and which set the conditions to buy. They could be on your website, in a leaflet or covered in conversation. We also crafted a value proposition. (Check out the one on the back of this book.)

Combined, all of this should make a compelling case for your customers to buy from you.

To contribute to your marketing, you will hopefully have crafted a choice of hooks. We looked at the moments when your customers would be at *their happiest* with your offering, and we picked up some advanced techniques for influencing your audience. We also looked at a simple five-part structure for designing collateral.

I also hope you found a way to make yourself *remarkable* so that people can talk positively about you behind your back, and a simple way for people to remember what you do.

In Psychology, they use the term 'Gestalt', which is German for 'form' or 'shape'. It is used in the sense that, when combined, ideas can take on extra meaning. The combination of ideas is worth more than the sum of the parts when totted up on paper. Like when you connect a locomotive engine to some carriages, their book value does not go up, but they are more useful to us. We saw it in action when we talked about intersectionality and making you remarkable.

The purpose of this workbook was to generate one or more 'Gestalten'. In other words, when your generated artifacts are placed in the context of all that you know, something is sparked off. If at any time you had a small surge of excitement when using this workbook, then it could be working.

Those people who start a business and carve their own path in the world are an awesome sector of society. You deserve our solid admiration, and I wish you every success.

David Chapple

Notes

1. Abraham Harold Maslow (April 1, 1908 – June 8, 1970) was an American psychologist who created Maslow's Hierarchy of Needs, a theory of psychological health predicated on fulfilling innate human needs in priority.

2. Paul MacLean (May 1, 1913 – December 26, 2007) was an American physician and neuroscientist who made significant contributions in the fields of physiology, psychiatry, and brain research through his work at Yale Medical School and the National Institute of Mental Health.

3. Daniel Kahneman (March 5, 1934 – March 27, 2024) was an Israeli-American psychologist best known for his work on the psychology of judgment and decision-making as well as behavioural economics, for which he was awarded the 2002 Nobel Memorial Prize in Economic Sciences together with Vernon L. Smith. Kahneman's published empirical findings challenge the assumption of human rationality prevailing in modern economic theory. Kahneman became known as the "grandfather of behavioural economics".

4. Geoffrey Moore (born 1946) is an American organisational theorist and management consultant, known for his book *Crossing the Chasm: Marketing and Selling High-Tech Products to Mainstream Customers* - the de facto handbook for anyone selling technology.

5. *Mad Men* is a TV drama series created by Matthew Weiner about one of New York's most prestigious ad agencies at the beginning of the 1960s, focusing on one of the firm's most mysterious but extremely talented ad executives, Donald Draper. (IMDb)

6. Robert Cialdini wrote the 1984 book on persuasion and marketing, *Influence: The Psychology of Persuasion*. It was based on three "undercover" years applying for and training at used car dealerships, fund-raising organisations, and telemarketing firms to observe real-life situations of persuasion.

7. Dennis Regan conducted the 'Coca-Cola Experiment' and published *Effects of a favor and liking on compliance* in 1971.

8. Jonathan Freedman and Scott Fraser published *Compliance without pressure: The foot-in-the-door technique* in 1966.

9. Stanley Milgram, Leonard Bickman and Lawrence Berkowitz published *Note on the drawing power of crowds of different size* in 1969.

10. Stanley Milgram published *Behavioral Study of Obedience* in 1963.

11. Tim Emswiller, Kay Deaux, and Jerry E. Willits published *Similarity, Sex, and Requests for Small Favors* in 1971.

12. Stephen Worchel, Jerry Lee, and Akanbi Adewole published *Effects of supply and demand on ratings of object value* in 1975.

Your Search Terms

Printed in Great Britain
by Amazon

62028031R10054